Banish Time M

T:ME
MASTERY

John McLachlan & Karen Meager

Time Mastery

First published in 2017 by

Panoma Press Ltd
48 St Vincent Drive, St Albans, Herts, AL1 5SJ, UK
info@panomapress.com
www.panomapress.com

Book design and layout by Neil Coe.

Printed on acid-free paper from managed forests.

ISBN 978-1-784520-99-1

Printed in Great Britain

Testimonials for Time Mastery

"After learning Time Mastery with Karen, our partners came away with productivity protocols we could implement in the practice straightaway. This makes us both productive and consistent as a senior team whilst still leaving space for our individual styles and ways of working. Really important for us as a growing business."

Janet Lewis; Partner,
JTP Architects, London

"By following Karen & John's methodology, leaders not only master their own time, they become an excellent efficiency role model for others. This improved everyone's productivity and results at EdenTree, allowing us to focus on our mission of delivering 'Profits with Principles' for our clients."

Sue Round; Head of EdenTree
Investment Management Ltd

"This book will help you make managing time an unconscious competence - leaving you space to get on with your life."

Melody Cheal; NLP Master Trainer, Author of *Becoming Happy*, Co-Author of *The Model Presenter*

"You can attend every time management course going and still not get back the fulfilment you seek from the hours that you spend. What Karen and John have done in *Time Mastery* is to unblock those things that will always undermine your best efforts if you do not address them. This book shows you, both conceptually and practically, how understanding your resources, your personal rhythm, and the way you communicate with others, you can enjoy an energised and productive life. You'll want to have a notebook to hand to get the most from this deceptively simple book. Do the structured thinking that Karen and John have laid out, and you will get more from this book than a lifetime of productivity courses."

Bryony Thomas; Author and Owner of Watertight Marketing Ltd.

Acknowledgements

We would like to thank Carys Tait, our illustrator, for understanding what we were looking for from the beginning and creating the wonderful illustrations we have in the book. Thanks also to our ever patient editor, Robert Watson, for his wisdom, good council and clear, Aussie style directness that has helped shape this book for the better.

A book is never just about the people who write it. It is a reflection of all the people that have informed and taught and worked with us throughout our careers and continue to do so. We want to acknowledge the influence, impact and support of our business colleagues, academic trainers, friends, family, students and clients past and present. You have all been, and continue to be, our teachers.

John & Karen

Table of Contents

Introduction

A Time Master is a master of their life. Being forever busy is not a sign of success. It is a reflection of being ineffective. Being a productivity ninja does not mean that you are living a successful and fulfilling life.

If you are busy living a full and satisfying life, that's a good thing. If you are busy and frustrated that you are not doing all the things you want to or you feel that your time is not your own, that's where time management isn't working for you.

This book is about being wise with what takes up your time. You will learn how to make good choices without feeling guilty and communicate that to others to win their support.

Lives are becoming busier and busier yet there are more labour- and time-saving devices available now than were available to our parents and our grandparents. Why is that? Why do we seem to have less time and so much competition for the little time we have?

People are not seeing time as a resource that they need to take care of and utilise. People see time as another thing to be managed, controlled and balanced against every other competing aspect of their life. This needs to change.

Your time is a precious resource and you can choose how to use it in pursuit of the life you want to live. Become a Time Master and use your own time resource for the things that matter to you.

Part A

Banish Time Management Forever

CHAPTER 1

It's About Time

"We have all the time in the world."

Hal David

Do you find that you do not have time to relax, focus as much on your career as you want to, watch your child play football or start that business you dream about?

Do you find that whilst you love your work life and love your non-work life you are constantly juggling them or feeling you should be spending more time on the other one?

The reason people have these challenges is because they have a number of things that are important to them and they are either making choices to try to balance all the competing things that are important or they are bouncing between them inefficiently.

People spend their time on the things that are important to them. This has much more to do with their deep-seated thinking and behavioural habits than their organisational skills.

Time "Management" is a myth. You cannot manage time; you can only manage your use of it. We are all individual and unique and your best way of using time is unique to you.

Time management tools help you consciously work out your priorities and actions, which takes effort. With Time Mastery you become unconsciously competent in the art of efficiency, so you don't have to think about what to do with your time or how to prioritise, you just do it because it's second nature.

Our clients complain that the problem they have with time management tools is that they take time and effort to use. They don't fit with how the client already thinks. Time Mastery enables you to design your approach to time that fits with your thinking. It also helps you to understand other people's time-related thinking, so that you can work more easily with them and set clear boundaries.

Time Mastery requires you to become clear on what is important to you in your life, eliminate time-wasting activity and align your everyday behaviour to create rhythm.

You sabotage your good intentions because your thinking habits, beliefs, values and habitual behaviours are personal to you. Time Mastery enables you to understand this, change your habits and thought patterns, and design a way of using and communicating your time that is unique and works well.

Time Mastery, not Time Management

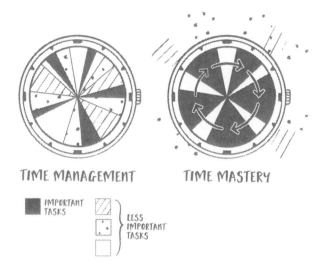

TIME MANAGEMENT   TIME MASTERY

IMPORTANT TASKS

LESS IMPORTANT TASKS

Time is an agreed measurement by which people make arrangements, interact with each other and plan and organise life. Many cultures still work in terms of daylight and dark, the seasons and moon cycles but for most of us that no longer works. As we evolved we needed more detailed measurements of time which, whilst helpful, have created unnecessary problems. We have allowed a useful organisational tool to take on a life of its own and have a level of importance that it should not have.

Time management suggests that time can be managed and controlled in some way but it's not a thing. It is an abstract concept that we all have different understanding of and beliefs around. Suggesting it is possible to control it is both unhelpful and counter-productive. It is like the wind or the sea. Yes we can utilise them and their energy; controlling them though, that is not so easy.

Look after your Life Resources

We all have three key resources in life: our Time, Health and Money.

The way people use their life resources and blend them together determines how successful and satisfied they are with life. The problem is that it can be easy to neglect a resource or use one in favour of the other. Focussing on Money at the expense of Time and Health is a common one.

People spend their time resource on what they think is important

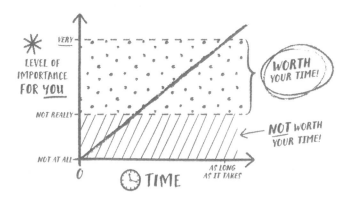

The fact that what you are doing is important to you does not mean that what you are doing is making you happy, successful or wealthy; that's not the point.

If you believe that working hard is important you will prioritise spending time on working hard over something else, like reading a book. If you believe that being home every night to make your kids their dinner is important you will prioritise time to do that over other things.

It may not be obvious why something you do is important to you; you don't procrastinate because you believe that procrastination itself is important, it's probably because getting it right, or not making a mistake is important to you. Procrastination is just the behavioural manifestation of the belief.

What you need to live a fulfilling life is for you to decide, no-one else. Time Mastery is not about being a super black belt productivity ninja, it is about doing the right things in the right way – for you.

CHAPTER 2

Look After Your Life Resources

*"I'd like to live as a poor man
with lots of money."*

Pablo Picasso

Time, Health and Money are your three Life Resources. They are the raw ingredients in your life, just like the ingredients required to make your favourite recipe.

Is that it? Just three Life Resources? What about relationships, skills, intelligence? If you are making a cake, it's a great cake because of both the raw ingredients you put in and the skills you have in putting them all together in the right order and in the right way. You need both. If you miss out a key raw ingredient, your cake will be a disaster no matter how well you construct it.

Relationships are not a Life Resource in themselves; you don't have a given right to anyone else's resources. Relationships can be highly beneficial for Time Mastery because you can pool your combined resources and get more done. First of all you need to develop these relationships, which takes time and energy. Energy is part of Health. In an organisational context, substitute Health for People; your people and their health are the Life Resource of the business.

Intelligence and skills are developed by combining Life Resources. You learn something new by investing Health, energy, effort and mental capacity with Time and perhaps Money. Learning happens through an investment in Life Resources which is how you get all the great skills and knowledge you have.

These are important; in fact they are critical to a successful life. They are just not a Life Resource.

You can overly focus on one resource at the expense of another; for example, sacrificing Health for Money. You can borrow from one to compensate another; such as using money to buy services that save you Time. When any of them run out completely you have a serious problem.

There is a relationship amongst them and when you talk about Time you need to consider the other two. It is the relationship and utilisation of all three that will help you live a fulfilling life.

Time is the continued progress and process of existence and events in the past, present, and future regarded as a whole. It is a universally accepted measurement. We all have the same number of hours in a day and days in a year to achieve the things we want to do. Time is a finite resource, once it is gone, it is gone. You cannot acquire more hours in the day.

Looking after all your resources requires training yourself to consider both the short-term and the longer-term impact of the spending, conserving and utilisation of those resources.

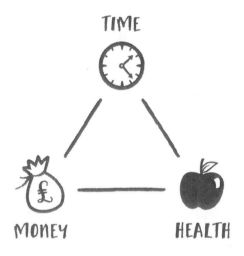

HEALTH AND TIME

Health is everything concerned with your physical body, your mind, spirit and energy. Without the appropriate level of health your ability to get things done and live your life fully will be limited. At an extreme, if you are dead you are dead and no amount of money will change that and time becomes irrelevant. Health is neither a finite resource nor an infinite resource. There are things you can do to improve your health, but as yet we have not found a way to live forever!

In organisations, replace Health for People. People are your resource so their health, energy and skills are important.

What are your beliefs around your health? Do you see it as something you need to look after or do you deal with problems as they come up? How much time do you spend on your health?

Health includes mental health and emotional wellbeing. Latest studies show one in three of us is suffering from some kind of mental health issue in our lives. Mental health issues and physical problems are not unrelated. It's no coincidence that people with mental health problems also have more physical ailments.

We all know our health is important. Despite all the knowledge and messages about it many people still seem to have behaviours that are detrimental to their health. Why is that? Why do otherwise seemingly intelligent people have behaviours that waste or damage their long-term health?

There are clear, logical and biological reasons why people don't invest in their health and pay attention to it. This is a result of how you have learned to view time.

Long-term needs, short-term behaviour

Few people think long term. Even fewer people relate it to the life they are living right now. People tend to worry and dream long term but don't do anything about it in the here and now.

Most humans are either focussed on short-term gratification or the avoidance of immediate pain. People may well look ahead to their old age but most of the energy and behaviour is focussed on dealing with short-term issues. Businesses may have five-year plans but the behaviour is short term and reactionary.

Life expectancy

This short-term focus makes sense, biologically.

In 1900, the average life expectancy for men was 47 and for women was 50. In 2014, life expectancy had increased significantly to 80 for men and 83 for women. In little over 100 years, life expectancy has nearly doubled and many scientists believe that the first people who will live to 150 have already been born. Humans have been on this Earth for thousands of years and only in the last 100 has there been such a significant increase in our physical life expectancy.

Great news and it would have been even better news if our thinking had changed to keep pace with this change, but it hasn't.

The key elements of our brain development have not changed significantly over the last few thousand years let alone the last 100. Is it any wonder that our brain's habits related to long-term thinking are struggling to catch up?

Why did men in Rome want to be gladiators given the high risk of death? Life expectancy was only 29 for men at the time so for them it wasn't a massive risk, and the rewards if they survived were huge. If your life expectancy was only 29 you'd have a completely different attitude to your life, planning and how you use your time than if it was 150.

Money and Time

By Money we mean the ability to trade something to obtain things we need and for most of us this is Money. Money is neither a finite nor infinite resource. It is possible to acquire more of it but in reality Money will never be infinite. Our capacity to earn and retain will not last forever.

Everyone needs things in life to survive, give pleasure, save time and maintain good health. Money is a flexible resource and can be used to obtain goods and services, experiences and even knowledge if you are willing to invest some time resource as well. It's no wonder it is so popular!

Money is one of the top five contributing factors to stress or depression, and worrying about it impacts your health. Arguments about it are the number one reason for relationship issues. Judgments are made about people who have it and don't have it and it impacts your life chances and status.

Short-term behaviour for long-term benefit

People are more likely to buy their kids disposable presents now to make them happy than invest so that they can go to university or have a deposit for their first house. Saving £25 a month over eighteen years would create £8,000 with a 4% growth rate. Some people do not think it is worth saving £25 each month, others do not believe that they can afford it and yet how many people regularly buy a takeaway coffee each working day which will easily add up to more than £25 per month?

Small changes in your lifestyle make a huge difference. It's because many of us boom and bust on our resources that we can't find rhythm. People spend on credit cards then can't afford to go out because they have too many bills – boom and bust. They work like mad for 11 months of the year so that they can take that holiday abroad – boom and bust. By finding more of a rhythm with all your resources you can both preserve and protect them whilst spending on things that really count.

When it comes to identifying where to spend your money take our Joy of Purchase test. If you feel a warm glow every time you put that cashmere jumper on then it was probably a worthwhile purchase. If the joy of purchasing ends at the till, then it's a good idea to look at your spending habits as they are not bringing you joy.

Cash rich, time poor

If you have enough money but are time poor, consider how you can use your money to buy you more time. You can employ skilled people to do the jobs you don't enjoy doing. This could be cleaning, ironing, diary management, cooking, gardening or managing your finances.

To do this and really value the time you have bought, you will need to relinquish some control and leave things to the people you choose. If you have what people sometimes call "very high standards" this can be a challenge, but what is more important to you: your time for other things or your idea of perfection? Often though people want both and that is unrealistic and a waste of time and money. In addition, if it creates stress for you then you are wasting all three of your life resources unnecessarily.

It is because money is such a versatile resource that people tend to value it so highly. However not everything can be bought and the pursuit of money at the expense of health and time is something people often regret later in life.

Think enough rather than more

Instead of thinking about what you want or need in terms of money, think in terms of what is "enough". Enough covers what you need and want to live a satisfying and fulfilling life. It is not abundance in terms of money being infinitely available. How much is enough for you and your needs? If you sit down and think this through, discuss it with your friends or partner you may be surprised at what enough really looks like for you.

Many clients, once they have clarity on what enough is for them, have dramatically amended their priorities and needs. The changes they have made have allowed them to focus their resources and channel them into the right things for them. They still have nice things, things that bring them satisfaction and joy. They are healthier and spend their time on things that contribute to their life, rather than limiting it.

Your resources, your life

Most people can do the short-term consequences fairly easily; it's the long term they have an issue with. The further away the timescale the less easy it is to predict. That is intellectually obvious but people's brains, not to mention businesses and the stock market, are not big fans of unpredictability. The tendency is to get a little edgy about this and as a result focus more on short-term, easier to predict actions even if they do not support their longer-term goals.

What time habits could you develop that would help you to look after your Life Resources more effectively? Sometimes an investment in time is exactly what is needed to support your other resources and the added bonus is it is likely to save you time later on. These could include:

- Time to heal after an injury or illness (spend time to look after health)

- Time to exercise (spend time to look after health)

- Time to research and identify a professional financial advisor (spend time and money to save time and money later)

- Time and money to train in a new career or acquire skills (spend time and money now for time, money and health later)

- Time to make something rather than buy (spend time to save money).

When you understand these concepts it opens up a world of possibilities for you and puts you in charge of your resources.

Are you as healthy as you want to be? If not what small steps can you take to build up that resource? If your money resource is not what you want it to be, what can you do to change that? How can you make more of your time your own?

Overnight you will not become a multi-millionaire athlete who has all the time in the world. However, with practise, effort and a focus on the long term you can make the small changes that will make a huge positive difference to your life.

Summary

What have you learned in this chapter?

- Your three Life Resources are Time, Health and Money.

- How you blend these three resources creates the life you have.

- Life expectancy rates have significantly increased in the last 100 years.

- Our brains still think in terms of short-term gratification and problem solving.

- Small changes can have long-term benefits.

Time Mastery comes when you can easily and automatically make the appropriate choices for all three of your resources. Decide where you want to begin working with this in your life and career.

Action: Think about this and if you have a notebook available write down:

- Your current attitude to Time, Health and Money.

- How is this attitude best reflected in your day-to-day life and career?

- What recurring problems are you most frustrated about that you now realise are a result of your short-term thinking?

From what you have thought about or written down, decide what you believe is the key change you will make to take control of your life resources.

Whatever you decide, begin now and the older you will thank you.

Time Myths

"Myths which are believed in tend to become true."

George Orwell

Myths are widely held, but lead to false beliefs or ideas. They are needed for writing a good story; not as much use when you want to live your life well.

Colin's realisation

We have been doing a coaching programme for a senior leadership team of a multi-national manufacturing company that is going through a change process. One of the key challenges facing the business during this change was that people were defending existing behaviours, ideas and processes as 'essential and key to the success of the business and what makes us who we are'. One of the coachees, who was becoming exasperated by the resistance summed up the power of and the issue of myths brilliantly when he said, "We have said the same things for so long now that most people believe they are true yet there is not a shred of evidence to support them".

That's the problem with myths: if you repeat them often enough and choose to look no further, they become truths.

As you read this chapter think about the beliefs and ideas you have about Time, about how you spend your time and about how other people spend their time. Are they useful? Do they stand up to any level of dispassionate scrutiny?

What are your myths?

Everyone has their own myths about time that they've collected from various sources through their lives, made them into facts and then relied on them to decide how to spend their time.

The problem is, these myths have never really been tested or evaluated for their impact on your life. You adopt behaviours in your life without ever questioning these myths because it's just the way it is. They have simply been accepted as true and then applied in your everyday routines.

Myths are over-simplifications of what is really needed and by understanding the complexity of your own psychology and beliefs around time you can take an important step forward in your goal of Time Mastery.

Time myths can suck the energy from you; they waste so much of your time and you don't even know it. It's time to unmask these pesky little myths and deal with them.

Myths and reality

When the myths are gone you have clarity. Clarity brings reality to any task or situation and allows you to spend only the time you need to achieve the task at hand.

There are four myths that we hear and see most when we are working with individuals and organisations.

The Four Common Time Myths

Myth 1 - Multi-tasking is a good thing

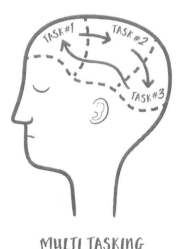

MULTI TASKING

Your brain can only focus on one thing at a time. To do something well you need to focus your full, present attention on it. Focussing your full present attention on what you are doing is a key aspect of Time Mastery.

What is called multi-tasking is actually your brain flicking from one thing to another so that each task gets a bit of your attention and the processing power of your brain. If you have many things on the go at once then you can't be very focussed on any one of them. You will divide your focus over a number of things and none of them will get your full attention. When someone thinks they are multi-tasking their brain is actually trying to track and deal with a number of different thoughts and activities in their mind at the same time. This drains your energy and reduces your thinking capacity. People multi-task because it 'feels' productive, rather than being an objective analysis of results and output.

For regular, small or trivial tasks, that may not be a significant issue though it has the potential to make every one of the things you are doing take longer.

For more complex tasks, multi-tasking will inevitably result in each task taking longer and may have the added effect that you will make more mistakes, miss things or do an incomplete job that needs to be reworked.

Multi-tasking may work when you are doing tasks that you are unconsciously competent at, that are routine and no-one else is impacted. Multi-tasking does not work when tasks are not routine, they relate to other people around you, or you need to give them conscious thought to achieve.

Driving is a good example of where you can more easily allow your brain to flit from task to task without significant reduction in the quality and time taken to do the driving itself. This is possible because driving is so automatic to most people. You will have noticed what happens if you are driving an unfamiliar car or in an unfamiliar place – it becomes much more difficult to drive and talk or drive and drift off somewhere else as you need to concentrate more.

Imagine trying to write a report, whilst thinking about dinner and then deciding to take a call. Is it any surprise that the report takes longer than it would have done if you'd turned off your phone and focussed on it? Perhaps the quality of the report suffers and you need to spend more time to rewrite it. The call may not get your full attention either which could waste even more time.

Examples of when multi-tasking doesn't work include:

Spending time with your kids whilst still thinking about work

You are not connecting with your kids and they will pick up on that. You will not experience the joy of that time together either. It's also unlikely that the work thinking you do will be of that great a quality.

Cooking dinner whilst on the phone

This has an impact on how the other person feels about you and the conversation as they know you are not giving them your full attention. Dinner may also suffer.

Focus your attention on the thing that needs to be done and make time for the other things later. Try it out for a day. Spend a day focussing on one thing at a time and notice how much more efficient and effective you are.

Myth 2 - Being busy is a good thing

"Busy" has become a word so packed with meaning in social circumstances that it is driving people to be busy fools.

Are you being active for a purpose that is helpful and moving you forward? Too often people are busy for the sake of being busy. They "need" to keep busy but is that busyness actually needed? Does the washing up really need to be done the minute you have finished your meal? Just because you always have a meeting on a Monday and it lasts an hour does not mean you should keep doing it.

The attraction of using the word "busy", psychologically, is to communicate to other people one of the following messages:

- I'm very important and in demand

- I'm very popular

- I'm very skilled

- Don't give me any more work

- Whatever you are about to ask me to do the answer is likely to be *no*.

When you describe yourself as busy, you are also communicating to yourself one or more of the following:

- I'm overloaded

- I'm not sure I can cope

- I have no space

- I'm bad at managing time

- I'm disorganised

- I feel a bit out of control.

Any of these will create an unhelpful feeling inside you around how you spend your time. If someone is too busy, it is not a badge of honour. It is an indication that they are finding it hard to prioritise and manage their life.

All activity should have a purpose for you. Consider instead describing your activity as being stimulating, interesting, efficient or any other more psychologically helpful way to focus your attention.

Myth 3 - The amount of time you spend thinking about something defines how important it is

People take time to think about something when they're not sure or need more information, rather than because it's important. When something is very important to someone and they are sure about it they often have such clarity that they spend less time thinking about it.

When you bought your dream house or car how long did you spend thinking about it beforehand? For most people this decision is made in the first 20 seconds. When the love of your life asked you to marry them, how long did you spend thinking about it? Chances are you instantly said *yes*. When someone close to you was ill and asked for help how long did you spend thinking about it? That's right: no time at all. When you saw your perfect job advertised, how long did you take to decide to apply for it?

People often take more time on things through fear, uncertainty and concern about other people's judgment rather than importance.

This is particularly true in organisations where a lot of time is wasted gathering more data talking about how important the decision is. Often this time is simply wasted and only taken to justify the route you want to take.

If your thinking style is causing you to procrastinate, ask yourself what is really stopping you. Do you need more information? Do you need another opinion? When you can identify what it is you actually need, you move decisions forward.

Myth 4 - Time management tools work for everyone

People think differently and have different beliefs and if they have a problem with that thinking, no time management tool in the world will solve it. A time management tool will only be effective where it matches the way people think. They can help people get organised, create clarity on what needs done and help to achieve things. That is true for some people some of the time but time management tools themselves do not lead to Time Mastery.

	Urgent	Not Urgent
Important		
Not Important		

Stephen Covey's Urgent/ Importance matrix from *The 7 Habits of Highly Effective People* is an example of an excellent time management tool that we use in our leadership development programmes. The interesting debate always comes when the group is discussing what each person means by the words Urgent and Important. For some people everything is urgent or its urgency might depend on who's asking for it to be done. For some people important is based on a set of criteria or it could be to do with what they love and feel is important. The truth is that these words are highly subjective and so the success in the application of Covey's method depends on how you define these words. Your definition will depend on your upbringing, your deep strategies for getting things done and your beliefs and values.

To achieve Time Mastery you need to go beyond the surface and consider your existing strategies and identify those that might be unhelpful.

Summary

What have you learned in this chapter?

- Myths are widely held, but false beliefs or ideas.

- Your time myths do not stand up to scrutiny yet have not been scrutinised.

- They are deeply held and often unconscious.

- There are four main ones that you need to eliminate from your thinking.

Action: Think about this, or use your notebook and write down:

- Which of the four Time Myths in this chapter have you always believed?

- What other Time Myths can you now identify having read the chapter?

- If you are not yet sure on the answers to the above then pay attention to your words and behaviour over the next week. What do you do or say that you now realise has no basis in fact?

From what you have thought about or written down, which is the key myth that you need to start working on to help you improve your use of your time resource and avoid wasting time?

Time Myths can seriously damage your use of time. When you let go of myths that do not help and use your time resources wisely you will gain more control of what you do and how you spend your time.

Imagine what it would be like if you stopped pretending to be effective as a multi-tasker and you focussed your time on the things that were important to you. How much more successful would you be and how much more would you get done?

What if you stopped being forever busy and became forever efficient? What if you thought less and did more and what if you spent less time creating to-do lists and spent more time doing?

You are no doubt already thinking about your time in a different way.

CHAPTER 4

Stop the Time Wasters

"Most people spend more time and energy going around problems than in trying to solve them."

Henry Ford

Time Wasters are common, everyday things that, with a little bit of focus and effort, can easily be changed, freeing up more of your time for the things you really want to do.

When you eliminate the Time Wasters from your life, you will have more time to focus on the things and people that are really important to you.

What a waste

Time Wasters are the things that you do that are unnecessary, do not help achieve what you want to achieve or are inefficient.

If something you are doing isn't necessary, doesn't achieve anything or is going the long way round then why are you doing it? Because you are human.

There are two key reasons why people do things which are unnecessary, do not achieve anything or are inefficient:

1. You copied others as a child

Children copy significant people around them, mainly parents; it's how humans learn and it's natural. As a child you weren't able to critically evaluate whether what you were copying was a really good or a really inefficient way to do the thing.

It was all you knew and you assumed that because someone bigger than you was doing it, it must be the right way. As a result of copying others, we all collect ways of thinking, beliefs and automatic patterns that have a strong influence on how we think and behave now. Unless we become aware of them and choose to do something about it.

You also copied different things from different people. This can create time-wasting issues as at times these different ways will clash and cause you to become stuck. For example, if Mum was a quick decision maker and Dad considered things slowly and carefully, there's a chance you'll have picked up both skills. You didn't have the cognitive skills to assess which decision-making skills suited which circumstance best, so you probably do a bit of both, or swing from being paralysed to being impulsive.

Happiness and success are not about choosing one way or the other; it is about choosing a way that works best for you and for the context you are applying it in.

2. Your bad time-wasting habits get OK results

The other way we generate time-wasting habits is that they work – kind of. The process might be painful, frustrating or distressing but, eventually, you get there.

Consider two examples with different strategies.

Your present-buying strategy

Do you start thinking about Christmas in July? You buy something, wrap it and put it away ready for the big day. Maximum organisation and efficiency. Gold star!

Why would anyone do that? Surely better to leave it until Christmas Eve, buy what is still available, run home and find any old paper (Happy Birthday will do) and then hours later, when the mammoth wrapping marathon is over, you collapse into a chair to relax and realise it's bedtime. Success!

Perhaps you agonise over buying your partner a birthday present but when you eventually choose (after asking 4000 people and having sleepless nights) they love it. Success!

Which one of these strategies wastes less time?

It depends on your point of view. In each case a present was bought, so the outcome was achieved. Yet is spending time in July thinking about Christmas a good use of time? Is rushing around at the last minute, creating stress and not necessarily getting what you want better than spending time with your friends and family? Would you have made the same choice of present if you had simply gone with your gut and avoided wasting so much time?

Your meeting-preparation strategy

Are you always prepared because you never know what is going to happen or what you will be asked? You spend three days before the meeting getting everything ready and there was nothing that you were asked that you were not prepared for. Success! They only asked three things; the other twenty-seven you had prepared for as well never came up.

or

You don't bother preparing as you never know what will come up and anyway, you'll be able to wing it. The meeting goes well, you wing it and no-one notices. Success! Nothing comes out of the meeting so it is a complete waste of time but at least you didn't waste any time preparing for it.

Both strategies get the result and both also waste time.

The Magnificent Seven Time Wasters

Time Waster #1: Thinking or talking about things that you cannot influence or control

If you were to monitor your thoughts and record your dialogue, how much of your energy is channelled into topics that come into this category? For every second spent thinking or talking about something you cannot control, you are taking time away from thinking or talking about things that you can do something about.

Topics that could fall into this category include:

- Gossiping or news sharing

- Complaining about something to someone who cannot or will not do anything to resolve it

- Dropping hints, making side comments and other undercover ways to try and influence someone

- Arguing a view or position to someone who doesn't care or can't validate it.

When you are sharing news, catching up or talking about other people in any context, ask yourself, 'Why am I doing this?' If you are discussing someone else in order to help you work out how to best engage with them, this could be productive. If you are simply moaning and plan to do nothing with or about the information you are sharing then it is wasting time.

Some people gossip or talk about irrelevant things to build and keep relationships. All the way back in history exchanging news was a way of connecting and reconnecting as human beings. It's why we still discuss the weather at length to new acquaintances – in the UK anyway! If it has a useful purpose for you, a genuinely useful purpose, then it may not be a time waster.

The key is to be clear on what that purpose is and then ask yourself whether it is worth your time.

Time Waster #2: Fantasising about the future (positively or negatively)

There's a difference between this and visualising goals or a positive future. The difference can be determined by asking yourself two questions:

Is what I am thinking about realistic?

Am I going to do anything about it?

Visualising goals is a very powerful process if the goal is one you aim to achieve and if you are prepared to do what it takes to get it.

If you dream about living in a massive house by the sea but have no plan of action and no intention of doing anything to get it, then it is a fantasy. Fantasising is not only a waste of time, it can also negatively affect you emotionally. If you are always thinking about wonderful things that never happen, your brain is constantly being set up for disappointment.

The same is also true of negative fantasising. Thinking about negative possibilities doesn't make you any better able to deal with them should they happen, so why distress yourself? Your brain is an amazing resource and it reacts better to emergency situations if it hasn't been programmed with lots of fake negative scenarios in the past.

Fantasising positively or fantasising negatively become thinking habits. You don't always consciously start them, you may just realise you are doing it. Breaking this habit takes practice and the best way to do it is to interrupt the fantasy and go do or think about something else. Do another task, take a walk, make a cup of coffee – anything that will interrupt the pattern.

This is not always easy as your brain can get addicted to those thoughts, even if they are negative. Mindfulness and meditation are really helpful for breaking these thought habits.

Time Waster #3: Going over, in your head, conversations or situations that have already happened

Your brain has a tendency to bring up unsatisfactory situations again and again and make you remember them.

The positive intention of this is for you to learn from them and inform your future behaviour. If you are used to ruminating in this way, your brain will keep reminding you, often in the middle of the night when you want to sleep!

Pay attention to the learning your brain is trying to give you. Is it always confrontational situations you could have done better in, or situations where you weren't as kind as you could have been? If there is something you want to do differently then go and learn how to do it. Once you take action your brain will calm down because it knows you are listening to it.

Next you need to break the thinking habit itself by interrupting it and doing something else, and with practice you will do this much less.

Time Waster #4: Doing activity without a clear outcome for you

Unhelpful habits creep in over time and that stops you from using your time well. Take a look at your habits and ask yourself, 'What does this get for me?' Typical activity that has no clear outcome includes checking your phone or email every five minutes, watching TV you are not really interested in and some chores that are done habitually.

When you aren't clear on your purpose then your brain just gives you habits as the next best thing. Which ones do you want to keep and which are you ready to change?

Time Waster #5: Having too many open loops at one time

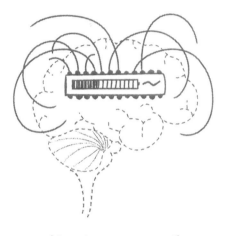

"TOO MANY OPEN LOOPS"

Open loops are ideas, activities and decisions that you have started or opened but haven't completed or closed. The minute you think about something you open a loop.

People often start things and don't complete them, or start a decision-making process and don't make a decision, or have an idea that they never take forward or close down. Having too many of these loops open is like having too many applications running on your computer: it drains the battery and impacts processing. People become exhausted by having too much open in their minds.

Instead of getting frustrated or upset by them take some steps to close them by:

- Taking action.

- Deciding when you will deal with the thing and close the loop until then.

- Deciding actively to stop something (and actually doing that!).

- Deciding actively to put something off and start it later. It helps to give yourself a date to pick it up again.

Some of you will be very imaginative, constantly coming up with new ideas and thoughts. Keeping an ideas book or somewhere you can log ideas to come back to when you have space is an excellent way of preventing your creativity from driving you mad, and wasting your time. Closing some loops will give you much more energy and brainpower to focus on what is really important.

Time Waster #6: Over-thinking without taking action

If something runs around your head without taking you forward then this is a waste of your time and your energy.

Take some action on the thing you are thinking about as this will help to change your feelings about it and help you to think about it differently. Small steps forward make a big difference.

Time Waster #7: Believing 'perfect' exists

Perfectionism is the enemy of success. Nothing is perfect, no relationship, job, piece of work or life. When you talk about perfection what do you mean? The definition is important.

Many people use the label "perfectionist" when describing themselves and often they are talking about having high standards. There is nothing wrong with high standards. Why wouldn't you want that if it motivates you and brings you joy in life? The challenge and the time wasting come when perfection becomes an obsession, as then the obsession for perfection will stop serving you.

When people are waiting for the perfect – whatever it is – they waste time and lose the opportunity to grow something or develop something. Some will keep waiting for the 'right' thing to come along before they get moving and for others they will keep on striving for the 'perfect' rather than being content with what is needed for success. If you're not sure whether this applies to you ask yourself whether your definition of perfect works for you? If it does then you probably have a healthy definition of perfect; if you are still waiting for that perfect partner or job to come along, then it probably doesn't.

Moving from Time Wasting to Time Mastery

Everyone needs some downtime and there are times when it is appropriate to put your brain in a jar and watch some rubbish on the telly. Sometimes you are discussing other people because you want to better understand what you can do to improve a situation or help someone. And what is wrong with a bit of escapism and dreaming about marrying your favourite film star or living a billionaire lifestyle?

Consider though how you spend your time, how much of it is productive and ask yourself the uncomfortable question, 'Where do I waste my time?'

There are also times when it may feel like time wasting but it isn't. If you are unwell and take time to recover and that means that you are not at work, can't go to that party, or leave the house, is that time wasting? *No.* It is spending time to recover your health, and that is a good use of time.

What about when you are delayed at an airport or anywhere else like that? If you are efficient and mastering time you could spend that time reading a book, phoning a friend for a chat or reading a report. This focussed and considered approach is an efficient use of time.

Summary

What have you learned in this chapter?

- People learn by copying, rather than evaluating and choosing best practice.

- Even when you get results you can still waste time.

- Time wasters are often unconscious habits and beliefs you may not even recognise as a time waster.

- There are seven major time wasters.

- Identifying your own time wasters enables you to decide how best to change your behaviour to stop them.

Action: It's time to eliminate your time wasters from your day-to-day behaviour. Think about this, or use your notebook to write down:

- What did you model as a child that you may now realise is inefficient?

- What do you do that gets a result, that you or someone else thinks wastes time?

- Which of the Magnificent Seven Time Wasters do you do and what strategies can you immediately think of which will help you reduce them?

From what you have thought about or written down, decide what you believe is the key change you could make that will make the most positive difference for you.

There is a psychological challenge to stopping doing something. When you want to stop doing something you end up thinking more about it as your brain keeps bringing it to your attention. This is why stopping eating chocolate is so hard. Your brain is still thinking chocolate, chocolate, chocolate, even though you don't want it to.

The way out of this loop is to focus on something else. To begin to eliminate time wasters from your day-to-day behaviour do something else instead of the time-wasting behaviour.

In the next section you will learn a set of skills, attitudes and practical approaches that you can use to achieve Time Mastery. The four Keys to Time Mastery are:

- Resolve Your Internal Conflicts

- Chunk Your Time for Success

- Think Rhythm Not Balance

- Communicate Your Time Boundaries.

You can approach them in any order. They are simply written in this order in the book because it's the most sensible way to learn and understand the ideas and concepts. Read through all the Keys first and then use Part C to help you plan where to focus your attention.

PART B

The Four Keys to Time Mastery

CHAPTER 5

Resolve Your Internal Conflicts

"The greatest conflicts are not those between two people but between one person and himself."

Garth Brooks

An internal conflict is where two (or more) things are important to you and they are competing for your time. This competition results in you draining your time and energy.

Have you ever said to yourself, 'I would love to sit down and relax but I need to get this done first?' Perhaps it's 'I really love my job but it's getting in the way of me spending time with my kids'. Both of these are examples of internal conflicts.

What common ones do you use or hear?

Time is wasted either in worrying about one of them whilst trying to do the other or trying to balance them off against each other. You end up doing neither very well and being less satisfied overall.

Identify your competing needs and find ways to use your time well and you will avoid waste in the worry or competition.

When you resolve internal conflicts you not only feel better, more relaxed and in control, you are also much clearer on what you are doing and that makes doing what is important to you much easier. Who doesn't want that?

Why we have internal conflicts

CONFLICT #1   CONFLICT #2

Life would be delightful and very simple if we could just do the things that give us pleasure and avoid the things that cause us pain.

Human beings are more complex than that.

Internal conflicts develop naturally as we grow up creating problems for us as adults. They are not the function of a problem childhood, a one-time event or some other misfortune. They are created because the people around you as you were growing up, usually your parents, are different from each other. That's all. They have different views, attitudes, priorities and beliefs. In relationships opposites often attract, so it is likely that they had some very opposing views on some things. As a very young child you pick up on these and begin to integrate them into your own personality.

Let's look at an example of how internal conflicts manifest in everyday life.

Gillian's internal conflict

Gillian's dad let her decide which games to play or where to go at the weekend; he would just go with the flow. Her mum was more disciplined, making sure Gillian did her homework every night and stuck to her bedtime routine. Gillian didn't dislike either approach, it was just the way things were. The problem came when as an adult she was trying to decide whether to put in some extra work on a project or take the day off and go out with her friends. Having internalised both ways of doing things she had not learned a time-efficient technique to deal with this conflict so what did she do?

Gillian found herself doing the following at different times:

- Thinking about it for a long time, looking at the project and trying to work out what would happen if she left it until the next day.

- Speaking to her friends to find out about the day out to decide if she really wanted to go.

- Doing one whilst regretting not doing the other.

- Deciding to stay home and work on the project but not do a very good job because once she got started, she realised she wasn't really in the mood.

Your mind can be running these competing priorities without you knowing it consciously. It is constantly balancing up 'should I be free flowing or disciplined and would it be better to do this now or that'. This all eats away at your time as well as your energy.

When you are clear in your own mind what is best for you, these decisions are not an issue.

Conflicts can cause dissatisfaction in your life, making you miss out on your goals or leave you feeling exhausted at the end of a day or week.

Identifying your conflicts

Think about the day-to-day struggles you experience with prioritising and making decisions about what to do. Or think about why you are not living a satisfying life. What is the conflict, block or tug-of-war all about for you?

Below are the common internal conflicts people experience.

Internal Conflict #1: Freedom v Security

When people experience this conflict their choices and priorities are being assessed by whether this supports their need for freedom, to have infinite choices and their need for security and safety.

You might want to do your own thing in life but are scared you won't have enough other resources (usually Money) to give you the security you believe you need. In relationships you swing from the steady safe partner to the wild but unreliable one, and repeat!

If you are running this conflict you will spend a lot of time thinking about whether you have enough security and a lot of time dreaming about freedom-type experiences or regretting not doing them.

Internal Conflict #2: Me Time v Others

This will feel like a constant juggling act or trade-off between doing things you want to do for yourself and attending to the needs of others. You crave Me Time but feel guilty when you do it.

Working parents often feel that they do not have any Me Time because they are either working (to provide for the family) or giving their time to their children or family activities. You will feel selfish about doing Me Time activities and will feel like you are doing the 'right' thing in Others' activities whilst quietly resenting it.

Internal Conflict #3: Work v Relaxation

With this you will dream about relaxing when working and think about all the things you need to do when you try to relax. You struggle to be fully present in either and are never truly satisfied when doing either. People do this in quite extreme ways; for example working all hours for six weeks and then taking a big chunk of time off for a holiday or to recover.

Internal Conflict #4: Ideal Job v Family Responsibility

People with this conflict may experience similar thoughts and feelings to the Freedom v Security Conflict and Me Time v Others conflict but it is specific to their work and family. Perhaps they have a dream to work as a skiing instructor but cannot make that happen with their family commitments, or their partner may have an expectation of their earnings that may prevent them from taking a job they really want.

The family aspect of this is important because people with this conflict feel trapped and hog tied by their responsibilities whilst also feeling secretly resentful about not being able to follow their dream. They won't share it with anyone because that's not 'fair'. This brings them back to responsibility. It's feels like a no-win situation.

Internal Conflict #5: Independence v Intimacy

People with this find relationships a challenge. This has an impact because they spend too much time moving in and out of relationships and struggling with 'should I stay or go' type decisions. At the heart of it is an internal struggle between a part of them that craves Independence and part of them that craves Intimacy. Unable to have both, people with this conflict will either stay in unsatisfactory relationships or bounce between partners, but they are never content with their relationship.

This is also seen in people with their choice of career. They are looking to 'work for themselves' and then when they do they miss the connection with others they can get working in an organisation. They will, as with relationships, stay in an unsatisfactory job or bounce between jobs looking for the right answer.

Take some time now to write down your own conflicts.

Finding peace; resolving Internal Conflicts

In a family, a business or for world peace, at some point, the key to resolving any conflict is compromise and negotiation. This may feel like you have to give in, or give up on something; that's how people often feel about compromise.

The problem with internal conflicts is that whilst you are on one side of the battle, you reject or dislike the other side. In a Me Time v Others conflict you will think you are selfish for thinking about Me Time when you are doing Others. In a Freedom v Security conflict you will justify to yourself and others your position from wherever you are in the conflict. When in Freedom you will say, 'I'm so glad I gave up that job and I am now free to do what I want' and when in Security you will say, 'It feels good to know all my bills are covered'.

How do you do it?

Whatever the conflict, it can be resolved. You will need to be honest with yourself, and if it helps, talk it through with someone you trust and who will not look to solve it for you or give you the answer.

Resolving internal conflicts is a 3-step process where you identify the positive intent of each side, appreciate each side for what it is trying to do for you, and reach a compromise that will allow you to use your time more efficiently.

1. Ask yourself, 'What is the positive intention of each side?' All of your behaviour is trying to do something positive for you, even if it is going about it in an unhelpful way. You might get four or five things for each side. Trust what pops into your head when you ask yourself this; the answers can often be surprising, especially if it's the part of you that you don't like very much.

2. Recognise and appreciate each side of the conflict for its positive intention. Make it clear in your mind that you are not taking sides and want to help each side of the conflict. Doing this over time you will reduce the struggle and you will feel less resentful about the conflict, spending less time on it.

3. For some people this will be enough to bring about peace; if not then you will need to negotiate between each side to try out some compromises. Avoid compromises that divide up your time as this may worsen the issue; instead find things that can satisfy both sides. Look at your positive intentions; how could you meet the needs of both? There will be concessions but the overall outcome will be more positive. For example in a Me Time v Others conflict can you find something that you all enjoy doing? Or in an Ideal Job v Family Responsibility conflict, can you start to train for something that is closer to your ideal job, whilst maintaining your family responsibilities?

Be patient and keep refining until you find an approach that works for you.

Tom's time-wasting conflict

Tom had always dreamed of working for himself. He loved making things and was quite good at it. He had fallen into his job as an accountant by mistake; it seemed a sensible career. He had a good salary and everyone thought he was successful. Except Tom. He now had a young family and felt more trapped than ever and wasn't progressing in his career. He spent a lot of time dreaming and worrying.

1. Tom identified his conflict as an Ideal Job vs Family Responsibility conflict. On one hand he wanted to make practical and useful furniture

for people and on the other he wanted to provide for his lifestyle and family.

2. Positive intention of 'safe job' was: pride, accepted, valued (by family), respected, financial security. Positive intention of 'ideal job' was: creative, practical, loving every day, helping people.

3. Tom wrote down all these words and asked himself, 'What could I do that would fulfil all of these positives?' He also discussed it with his wife and they formed a plan.

Tom stayed at his accountancy job for another 2 years whilst he saved (fulfilling financial security), then stepped down to 4 days a week and began the training he needed to master his craft and learn how to run a business. After 3 years he ran a small bookkeeping business half the week and made and sold furniture the other half. His aim was to keep tweaking the work portfolio until it flowed easily and fitted well as part of his life.

Summary

What have you learned in this chapter?

- We all have internal conflicts.

- Internal conflicts are a normal part of growing up.

- Time is wasted because you can't easily resolve the competing priorities.

- Each side in a conflict has a positive benefit for you.

- Conflicts are resolved through negotiation and compromise.

- There is a 3-step process to resolving your internal conflicts.

Action: Now you have awareness of your own internal conflicts you need to do something with them. Think about, or using your notebook consider:

- What are your key internal conflicts.

- Which have the most unhelpful effect in your life and career?

- From what you have thought about or written down, decide what you believe is your key conflict to begin working on towards your own Time Mastery.

- Allocate time and use the 3-step process to resolve the conflict.

- At the end of a month review the changes that have arisen as a result of the resolution and identify any adjustments that you need to make to maximise the benefits of the change.

By resolving the conflicts you have identified in this chapter what could you do differently? What would you be able to achieve that you have so far failed to make happen?

Pay attention to your internal conflicts and decide now that you want to deal with them, stop wasting time and take action. The next time you hear yourself saying, 'I want to… but' or when you find yourself sitting at your desk looking at your screen and thinking about being at home, know that this is evidence of an internal conflict and that you can resolve it and reclaim your time.

CHAPTER 6

Chunk Your Time for Success

*"Everywhere is walking distance
if you have the time."*

Steven Wright

A time chunk is the period that you normally split your time into when thinking about tasks and activities. That period can be helpful or unhelpful depending on what you want to achieve.

Some people think in short time chunks: how much they do in an hour or even what they can they do in ten minutes.

Others don't really consider minutes or hours; they might think in half days, days, weeks, months or even years.

Whatever period of time you think in is your time chunk.

HOW WILL YOU CHUNK YOURS ?

Do you think about what you are doing today? If so do you split this into morning, afternoon and evening chunks, into hourly chunks or 15-minute chunks?

Do you have an understanding of the key things you will be doing this week, or over an even longer chunk of time?

Whilst there is not a 'best' way that works for everything and everyone, there are specific situations and contexts where a particular way of chunking time will be more efficient and help you use your time more efficiently.

Take the example of someone who thinks in terms of morning, afternoon and evening. They will:

- Be more efficient with tasks and activities that chunk neatly into those periods of time.

- Be less efficient doing a quick thing of less than an hour. They are likely to either put it off as it is not significant enough in their mind or take longer than they need to achieve the task.

- Have problems thinking about longer-term goals and ideas.

Take the example of another person who thinks in weeks or even longer. They will:

- Be more efficient with longer-term projects and developing ideas that will take time to achieve, where the steps needed are unclear or have to be defined as they go.

- Be less efficient doing smaller, what they see as insignificant, things that would make their life easier and be helpful in the long term.

Imagine then putting two people with those opposite time chunks in the same team, the same company, or even a relationship? Imagine a group of people with the same time chunk preference working together? Where would that result in an efficient use of time and where would it result in a lot of time being wasted?

In organisations, the chunking preference of the person or group in control of a project, team or even the organisation itself will have an impact on what it focuses on, how much time it spends on things and what it sees as important and not important.

Chunking time for success requires awareness of your own and others' time chunking style, the benefits and challenges of each and the ability to use the appropriate style for the appropriate task.

The 3 steps for Time Chunking Mastery are:

1. Identifying your time chunk preference.

2. Adapting your planning to suit your preferred way of chunking time.

3. Stretching your preference when the context requires it.

1. Identifying your Time Chunk preference

There are two elements to this: your chunking size and your chunking sort. Think about planning something or consider your week ahead: what springs to mind? Is it the key big events and milestones or does your mind give you details and specifics?

Chunking Size

Big Time Chunkers

They consider time in terms of key goals and milestones. They will have big ideas and big problems. Often great strategic thinkers, they have the ability to think in the long term and maybe even beyond their lifetime.

Really useful for:

- Thinking through consequences

- Decision-making around important life choices

- Keeping people and a project aligned with the bigger picture

- Ensuring wider and longer-term impacts and issues are considered

Not so useful for:

- Actioning the small measurable steps

- Appreciating the importance of the details

- Listening to problems being identified by others

Big chunk thinkers can also get overwhelmed by their problems. They have a big chunk worst-case scenario up their sleeve for every situation which can get them down when things are not going well.

They can also fool themselves by thinking that they have a lot more time available to do something than they really have, and can put things off or find things hard to start because 'one more day won't matter'.

Small Time Chunkers

They consider time in terms of days, hours or even minutes. They measure their efficiency in terms of how many things they can get done in a given timescale. Great at thinking about all the details, they are often seen as productivity demons, busying themselves with lots of things.

Really useful for:

- Checking details
- Accurately assessing how long something will take to complete
- Breaking down big projects or activities into manageable pieces
- Managing the day-to-day activities of projects

Not so useful for:

- Getting bogged down in details
- Obsessing and busying themselves with things that are not so important to the bigger picture
- Projects that need to be developed as they progress

Small chunk thinkers can be very accomplished worriers; the details bug them. This can be exhausting as it is not possible to solve everything.

They can also fool themselves into believing they have accomplished a lot when they have actually just done a lot of activity. Activity is only productive when it is in the service of achieving a purpose or a goal.

Chunking Sort

A chunking 'sort' is the way in which a person organises how they view and deal with the activity and tasks they have.

Time Sequencers

People who sort this way see in their mind a line of time and can easily place events and activities in the past, present and future. They will describe their day or week as a sequence: 'On Monday we did this … then Tuesday …' When organising anything their starting point will be to sequence the order of events or activities to achieve. They can make excellent project managers or consultants. Once they have a plan they will deliver it.

The downside for Time Sequencers is that it is hard to deviate from a plan once in place. They find it stressful and often resist it. Spontaneity and staying in the moment are more difficult because their mind is always sequencing moments and activities as part of a wider process.

Time Sequencers can be perceived by others as tedious, especially when combined with small chunk thinking. If asked, 'How was your day?' they will explain it in very small details and in order, and if they miss something out they will need to go back and start again!

Time Themers

These people have buckets in their head with different subjects in them. When planning a holiday, they may find themselves looking back over former holiday photos or browsing brochures looking at locations they have no intention of visiting simply because their mind is in the 'Holiday' bucket. Often inspiration or great ideas come from this way of thinking. Left field answers to problems can pop into their head when they are just floating around in the appropriate subject bucket. Time Themers are also great at being spontaneous, dropping what they are doing to focus on something else.

They will like things to develop organically and resist being made to do a process or follow a procedure. They prefer to see how it goes and explore. If you are not this sort then it will drive you nuts.

The downside for Time Themers is that they have trouble completing things. Their mind has probably wandered off a few times and is now elsewhere doing or thinking about something related but not the thing in hand.

They can be perceived as being vague and woolly, especially if this sort is combined with big time chunk sizes. They can also struggle with learning in conventional settings that are quite linear and procedural. They thrive in experiential learning environments that fit better with their way of sorting.

2. Adapting your planning to suit your preferred way of chunking time

People are not disorganised. That is a judgment made by someone else with a different chunk size and sort about how someone sorts and orders their lives.

You can be efficient regardless of the size of your Time Chunks and how you sort. Your way of doing this effectively will depend on what skills and tools you have picked up along the way.

Here are our top tips for you based on combinations of size and sort:

Big Time Chunker and Sequencer

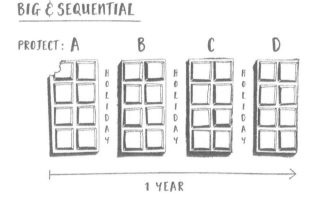

Group activities into key milestones in a sequence. For example list your key achievements or goals by month or even year.

Spend time ensuring your goals are clear and have target dates. This will give you motivation and focus.

Plan your breaks within the week rather than the day. People with this sort can work very intensively for days at a time then take a day or two off completely.

Big Time Chunker and Themer

Plan your activities in Themes rather than processes. For example, have an afternoon working on Marketing and just do whatever comes up for you around that theme.

Do detail and process only when you need to and don't spend too long on it in one go.

You will get easily immersed in things so when you feel your energy running out, take a long break from what you are doing, like going for a walk or a swim. It will refresh you ready for the next Theme.

Small Time Chunker and Sequencer

Break activities down into a chunk size you can look at and feel clear and motivated about doing.

Plan your day in hour-by-hour chunks as long as the activity has purpose.

Plan in your breaks throughout the day or you might not take them.

To-do lists work well for this type. Make them daily and enjoy ticking things off as you go.

Small Time Chunker and Themer

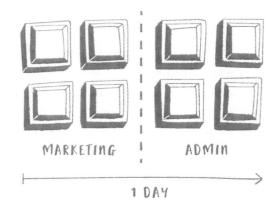

SMALL & THEMES

MARKETING   ADMIN

1 DAY

Spend small chunks of time working in Themes rather than processes or procedures.

Take breaks when you feel like it. More frequent shorter breaks work well for this type.

Use visual aids like mind mapping to work your way around your Themes.

By adapting your way of organising and planning to suit your preferences, you will be more efficient and the quality of your output improves. Work out the Time Chunk and sort of the significant people in your life, your boss, friends or partner to be able to communicate things to them in a way that meets their time sort. They will understand you better and feel reassured because in their minds you will be talking sense.

Jackie, Dean and Zoe: A Chunking Challenge

Jackie plans her life week by week and gets immersed in things. When doing the housework she will frequently end up spending hours poring over old photo albums she found whilst cleaning. She is a Big Time Chunker and Themer. Dean plans his day in hours, he considers himself a productivity demon, ripping through household tasks quickly, starting at the top of the house and working down. He is a Small Time Chunker and Sequencer. They laughed about their different approaches until they had a baby.

With Zoe's arrival their different approaches caused frustration, which when coupled with lack of sleep led to friction. When Jackie was caring for Zoe, she would immerse herself in the moment, cuddling her and playing with her. She loved this but found that very little else got done. Jackie also got overwhelmed by feeding as she only started preparing her food once Zoe was already hungry. Dean was quickly into the routine. He tried to help by making a feeding plan that Jackie could use, but she forgot to use it because she was so engaged in playing. When Dean took over he stuck to the feeding plan and routine as he felt it was important. Jackie felt inadequate and also resentful towards Dean. She didn't like his approach, as it seemed a bit regimented and impersonal.

The issue was not of one parent being better than the other; it was simply a difference in time chunking. Understanding this allowed them to compromise.

They stopped taking the other's behaviour personally and could openly discuss what was happening each week and what needed to be in Zoe's (hourly) routine to support that. Jackie agreed to go along with some of Dean's scheduling to make things smoother and Dean scheduled time to just spend with Zoe playing or reading, rather than thinking mainly about her immediate needs.

3. Stretching your preference when the context requires it

There are some important life areas that just don't suit a particular way of chunking and sorting time. In these areas if your time preferences are not suited you'll need to find a way to get around this. Let's look at two examples.

Example 1: Financial Planning

The Problem:

All time types (apart from Big Time Chunker and Sequencer) struggle with financial planning. Themers have a tendency to overspend, because they don't think about consequences until it's too late. Themers also can't think far enough ahead in life to get motivated to save for a pension for example. Those with a small chunk preference can't see the bigger picture and so don't save early enough or invest enough. Their spending and saving tends to be payday to payday or they can just about cope with saving for the next holiday, but no further.

The Solution:

- Accept that this is not your area of strength and get some professional help. Professional financial planning is not very expensive when you consider the overall impact on your life.

- Set up appropriate and useful financial habits and then forget about them. Decide to save a percentage of your salary, a certain amount each month or pay off that credit card. Set up a direct debit and then forget about it. By making it a habit and being disciplined you will set yourself up for success.

Example 2: Health and Fitness

The Problem:

The only time sort preference that is good for Health and Fitness is Small Time Chunker and Sequencer. A healthy diet and exercise regime needs small steps with a small amount of leeway for divergence from the programme. All the other preferences have a good chance of sabotage, even if healthy routines are started with good intentions. All Big Time types want big results and so won't be convinced of any changes in the time they are prepared to dedicate to it. They are also vulnerable to boom and bust patterns; for example extreme diets followed by periods of bingeing. Big Time Chunkers are likely to ignore signs of illness until it is very bad, and that may impact their ability to recover. All Themers can get very motivated by a new fad but get bored quickly or move onto another fad.

The Solution:

For Big Time Chunkers

- Take smaller steps in this context of your life. Set smaller goals and stick to them.

- Make small changes in your diet, one at a time until they become part of your natural rhythm and habit.

- Make small incremental increases in your exercise routine and stick to it.

- Big Time Chunkers and Sequencers can do well at exercise classes as it fits with their sequential preference. The key is not to start missing classes as 'one won't matter'.

For you these changes will feel very small so motivation to keep going is your main issue. At the time it won't feel like you're doing enough and at times you'll think, 'What's the point because it's not working'. If you get these thoughts, notice them and keep going; you are making progress.

For Themers

- Think about getting a personal trainer. This will align with your Theme style and if you can build a good on-going relationship with them they will do the small sequential process for you. You just have to turn up and do as you are told! You need to invest for the long term though because if it's only a short-term thing you are unlikely to keep it going for yourself.

- Get a job that keeps you fit. Anything outdoors or including more moving around will get you fitter without you having to think about it.

- Only have healthy food in the house and always give yourself a choice that you like. Themers hate not having choice; for example, if eggs or porridge are equally healthy and you like both, make sure they are both always available to you and then you are less likely to diverge from your routine.

Building a Project Team

A creative retail business we are working with wanted to build a project team that would blend efficiency and quality. They created the team using a combination of people with the right skills *and* time chunk sorts for the job. Everyone also had their day job to do so they couldn't dedicate all their time to the project.

For the beginning phase they selected creative people who were Big Time Chunkers and Sequencers to frame the project. Big Time Chunkers and Themers did the in-depth thinking on the scope and essential elements. Once defined at a high level, they brought in the Small Time Chunkers and Themers to define the criteria specifically and then the Small Time Chunkers and Sequencers to map out the project. Tag teams of a mix of time sorts kept overall charge of the project in the delivery phase and a group of people representing a mix of skills and time sorts came together at the end to sign it off.

This way not everyone was needed at every stage in the project. People were used where their skills could best be utilised and mixed teams were used to challenge the thinking biases of the others.

Summary

What have you learned in this chapter?

- People chunk time in different sizes and periods of time.

- Each different chunk size has attributes and creates problems.

- People sort time Sequentially or in Themes.

- Each style has attributes and creates problems.

- Understanding your preferences allows you to adapt how you plan and organise your life to best suit you.

- People are different, so understand and utilise this rather than judge it.

Now you know the foundations of chunking time you need to decide where you want to begin working with this in your life and career.

Action: Think about this, or use your notebook and write down:

- What are your preferences?

- The key skills and benefits that come from your time chunking preferences.

- Where are these preferences best reflected in your life and career?

- What recurring problems are you most frustrated about that you now realise are a result of your time chunking preferences?

Decide what you believe is the key action you want to take to begin working towards your own Time Mastery using Time Chunking.

You may want to take some time each morning to better plan your day. You may actually look at the week ahead, see what is involved and decide to allocate the time needed to achieve it, rather than rushing headlong and seeing how it goes.

Perhaps it's letting go of the need for all the detail just a little bit?

Notice the Time Chunks in others. When you are next sitting at that meeting listen out for other people's chunk size or sort. How is it different from yours and how do you react to it? When you are talking to your partner or friends what do you notice about how they chunk their time?

Chunking your time for success is a key to Time Mastery and now that you know it, take the steps (not too small and not too big) that you need to take to embed this in your life.

CHAPTER 7

Think Rhythm Not Balance

"Yesterday is gone.
Tomorrow has not yet come.
We only have today. Let us begin."

Mother Theresa

Rhythm is the ability to use your time efficiently to live your life, focussing on each activity, giving it the time it needs and when that time is over moving on to the next thing.

Top class performers, dancers and sports people all have rhythm; what they do flows and looks effortless. They have an economy of movement and as a result use their time as efficiently as possible. No wasted effort, no wasted time. If you observe the most successful people in any walk of life, they have this sense of rhythm: everything works together to deliver the outcome, nothing jars or conflicts, all movement is made in the same direction in service of their goal.

Time Mastery involves the same sense of rhythm and economy of movement.

Compare this with the word 'balance'. Balance is not efficient. When you seek balance you are looking to make an often arbitrary trade-off between two or more things in the hope of keeping things 'in balance'.

There is a lot of talk about balance: balancing the competing priorities, balancing the needs of the various stakeholders, work-life balance. Balance, and the desire to have it, creates competition for time that can often make you inefficient. You waste time moving between competing things, shifting focus and having to realign to each as you do.

You cannot balance your work against your life; that doesn't make sense. Work is part of your life and you decide, in the rhythm of your own life, how big that part is.

Let go of 'life as a trade-off'

Sadly far too many people live life as a constant series of trade-offs, with the hope of achieving some kind of overall balance.

BALANCE

Picture in your mind someone trying to balance. It could be someone balancing on a tight rope, or a seesaw or walking along wall. Imagine your life like that. You put a little on one side then, afraid of tipping too far, you put some on the other side, then go back to the other side. Time consuming, stressful and, ultimately a never ending battle. A waste of time.

Life as a series of trade-offs and compensatory actions creates, at best, neutrality. Why settle for that?

Simple changes create rhythm

As with much in life, it is small adjustments that are needed rather than radical changes.

You see some busy weeks ahead at work, and book in a few days holiday, or a trip out with the family as part of that. This is not as balancing compensation for being at work too much. Do it as a genuine activity, part and parcel of the rhythm and flow of your life. There is no need to justify either activity or apologise about one or the other.

The weather at the weekend is likely to be wet. You decide to change your plans and cut the grass tonight when you get home. The other planned thing can wait until the weekend as it is not weather dependent. That is a better and more efficient use of your time.

Your rhythm of life

We are all going against our own natural internal rhythms. People work longer hours than is sensible and take on more things than is healthy. Health issues around stress and depression are rising dramatically.

Whilst unexpected events and situations do happen and need to be dealt with, underneath it all the circle of life flows on with precision and predictability: the World's, Nature's and yours.

Everyone is unique and therefore you will have a natural rhythm that works for you.

Some people talk about being 'in the flow'; you may even have said it or felt it yourself from time to time. When you hear someone say this or when you feel it for yourself that is when you are at your best and this is part of your own natural rhythm. When you are in a natural flow, the tasks you are doing are easy and time either stands still or disappears. You lose track of it. Remember the feeling? How good does it feel when this happens? How much do you achieve? How stressed do you feel when you are 'in the flow'?

Being in rhythm has a little more to it than simply being in flow as it encompasses both the conscious and unconscious aspects of yourself. You need to be able to immerse yourself in something and not be late for work. You need to be able to challenge and stretch yourself whilst respecting your limits.

Finding your rhythm

1. Become aware of your energy thresholds

The challenge for many people is that they do not know, or they ignore, their own thresholds to the detriment of their time and their health. Doing something important with low levels of energy rarely goes well.

Your thresholds are unique to you. An activity that can really boost another person's energy can be a real drain on you.

Is your energy enhanced or drained when you:

- have lots to do or nothing to do?

- are with or away from unfamiliar people?

- are with or away from trusted close people?

- have structure or are free flowing?

- have clarity or a lack of clarity?

- are sitting still or moving around?

- have peace and quiet or hustle and bustle around?

In any family, relationship or organisation you need to be consciously aware that people are different and need different things. If your partner or child likes their own space and peace and quiet, give them it if you want them to thrive. In an organisation open plan offices work for some people but not for everyone. It does not mean anything about a person's competency or commitment; it is simply what gives them energy and what drains that energy.

Once you know where your thresholds are you can plan and organise life to take this into account, thereby creating rhythm in your life. For example:

- If loud social networking events drain your energy, you might decide that a maximum of two a month is enough. They may be important for your business meaning you can't avoid them completely so organise them in a way that works for you.

- If trusted, close people give you energy, can you arrange to see them more frequently? At times when there are a lot of draining events taking place you may want to see them more often to give you a little energy top up.

- If sitting still in a quiet environment recharges you, is there somewhere in your home or office you can go to get a little fix of this every now and then? Perhaps you can do this at planned intervals, like every time you have a break.

2. Invest in your relationships

Healthy relationships run easily, give you energy and make working or living together a joy. Unhealthy relationships are stressful, run as a trade-off, time is wasted second guessing each other and playing games.

Healthy relationships take effort, require you being open to change and compromise and having dedication to work through difficult situations. They run easily once they have been invested in.

Time invested in ending unhealthy relationships that are not working is also time well spent. These relationships take a lot of time and energy to maintain, without giving back. It's not about being unkind to the other person, or rejecting them. If it's not working, it's not working.

At work you don't always have a choice over who you work with. Wherever possible though, choose your boss and co-workers with care.

Never take a job, no matter how much it pays, if you meet your potential boss and know immediately you will never get on. Problems with workplace relationships is the number one cause of stress and mental health issues at work.

3. Use the Three Life Resources to support each other

LIFE RESOURCE-O-METER

Combine your Three Life Resources to create a rhythm in your life that works for you. For example:

Spend time now to save time later

Spend time (and maybe money) finding trusted advisers in life that save you time, energy and even money in the long term. These could include a friend, financial adviser, accountant, health professional, a coach, personal trainer. You can't do everything yourself. Accepting that is part of Time Mastery.

Invest time doing due diligence and checking out their credentials, being sure they can be trusted and are on the same wavelength as you.

Spend money to save time

If you spend time doing things that don't fulfil you, can you pay someone else to do it? There are excellent businesses out there designed to support busy people. This includes businesses to do your ironing, cleaning, gardening and organise your diary. This may be much less expensive than you think. Cost out what you need and then decide whether you are prepared to spend some of your money to give you more time. If you are moving house, can you pay someone to do it all for you. If you love holidays but not researching them, invest in a great travel agent. Any of these ideas can save you time and can often save you money as well.

Spending health now to save time later

Use this one sparingly and with caution. It is important to note that once our health, energy and spirit falls below a certain threshold it may not be retrievable.

For short-term projects or one-off events you may choose to push yourself hard to achieve something that will pay off in the longer term. This could be working longer hours to complete a project or coming home in the evening and working on a DIY project until late into the night, or even studying for a new qualification whilst working full-time as well.

Finding your rhythm won't happen overnight. It is a process of constantly refining and trialling things and then taking stock and seeing how they impact you.

Keep an eye on those energy thresholds and notice when you are getting near them. As you become more skilled at Time Mastery you may well find that your thresholds increase.

From Constant Juggling to Rhythm

Janet felt as if her life was a constant juggling act. She spent a few weeks doing an audit of her energy thresholds. She discovered two key things: her coffee catch up with her close friends gave her energy and taxiing children between loud play dates with parents she didn't know well drained her energy. She decided to make her coffee catch ups sacred and only moveable in emergencies (she had often cancelled them when seemingly 'important' things came up) and she took action on play date hell.

First she talked to her children to find out which of the play dates they really enjoyed, she prioritised these and made an effort to get to know the parents better. Because of this she felt she could negotiate some picking up and dropping off arrangements that meant less taxiing for everyone. She dropped the play dates that were less important and every time a new invitation came in she discussed with the children which they would prefer to attend, with a 'two a week' rule in her head. Sometimes it was more or less, but overall they stuck to it. Even with seemingly small changes Janet found an increase in her energy levels, enjoyment and feeling of rhythm in her week she hadn't experience before.

RHYTHM

Summary

What have you learned in this chapter?

- Balance is difficult to achieve and very difficult to maintain.

- Rhythm in your life will create flow.

- Your rhythm is unique to you.

- Understanding your energy thresholds is essential to Time Mastery.

- Invest in your key relationships.

- You can use your Three Life Resources to help create rhythm.

Action: To get you moving, here are the steps to take in developing your rhythm.

Review your last week and identify the times when you felt that you had rhythm and life was flowing:

- What was true at those times that is not normally true?

- What wasn't present or happening that normally is?

- What is there to learn from those times of flow?

For the next 7 days, think about your energy thresholds and:

- Notice what activities, people or events either add to your energy or don't seem to drain it.

- Notice what activities, people or events drain your energy.

- At the end of the 7 days decide on one step you can take that will help you with your energy threshold.

Considering the use of your Three Life Resources of Time, Health and Money:

- Make a list of the three most time-consuming activities you do in your day-to-day life.

- Which activity (or activities) could you spend money on to help better use your time resource?

- What is the likely weekly cost of spending money on this?

- When you look at the Time resource being consumed and compare it to the Money resource that you could use instead, how do you feel?

- Based on the above, what, if anything, will you do now?

From what you have thought about or written down, decide what you believe is the key action you want to take to begin working towards creating rhythm in your life.

The next time you are travelling home from work review your day and ask yourself how much rhythm you felt in the day. If the answer is not a lot then what can you begin to do to change that now? If the day flowed well then how can you replicate that in other contexts of your life or over more of the time you are at work? Once you have an idea of what you want to do, put it into action. The next morning, as you travel to work, decide what you are going to do differently and do it.

Rhythm is the key to the achievements of many successful people and when you find yours it will be the gateway to your own success.

CHAPTER 8

Communicate Your Time Boundaries (Part I): Behaviours

"Life seems but a quick succession of busy nothings."

Jane Austen

Your Time Boundaries are the way in which you demonstrate to yourself and others how you are willing to spend your time. You need to have boundaries: rules about what you will and won't do.

You will make better decisions because you will be in control of what you are doing, rather than being controlled by other people's needs. You will not waste time on things that are not important to the overall quality of what you are doing. People around you will know where they stand with you, rather than you running around trying to keep everyone happy.

You cannot not communicate

Each and every day you are training other people how to treat you by how you speak and behave.

A significant amount of communicated information from other people gets registered in your brain without you even really thinking about it.

Do you have some people in your life that you know you can be direct with and they will respond well to what you say? Do you have others you dread being direct and clear with? Are there people you know that you can always ask for help and be sure of getting it and others you wouldn't ask for help from in a month of Sundays?

It's unlikely that you've ever had an explicit conversation with that person outlining the rules of engagement. You haven't said to them, 'Are you a person I can ask for help?' They don't wear a badge saying, 'Please interrupt me any time you like' or one that says, 'Approach at your own risk'.

People communicate their boundaries through their words and actions in a less direct and yet equally clear way and your brain registers their behaviour. In the next chapter we will talk specifically about the language you use to communicate your Time Boundaries; in this chapter we are focussing on behaviour.

What are you communicating? Is it what you want to communicate? The problem is that you are often unaware of what your behaviour is saying to people about how to treat you in your everyday life.

You behave your Time Boundaries

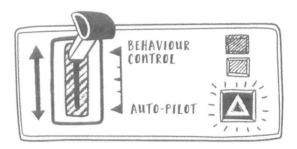

BOUNDARY CONTROL PANEL

When was the last time you got together with your friends and put the world to rights or the last time you engaged in gossip, news swapping or a good old moan? How often have you found yourself in the same old meeting with the same old agenda? You too!

Human beings have good reason to engage in these activities:

- Discussing world politics might improve your intellect or reasoning skills. You may also gain new information.

- Exchanging news and gossip is a way of relating to others or demonstrating your power.

- Having a good old moan can be therapeutic because it gets the problem off your chest – and you never know when someone might actually have the answer!

When you do these activities you are sending other people signals about what you focus on and how you spend your time. It is then difficult at some later point for someone to believe you when you say, 'I'm too busy to…'

There are common roles that people adopt in relation to how they behave their time. Each of these role types gives out a mixed message that is picked up by other people. The people may genuinely believe they are busy, but their engagement in common time-wasting behaviour gives other people a different and unhelpful message. This creates messy boundaries. It may also create an unhealthy culture where people have to buy into this behaviour and therefore everybody wastes time.

The Distractor

Mixed message: believes they are being engaging and friendly, other people actually feel frustrated with their lack of focus.

This role engages in behaviour that stops themselves and other people focussing on what's important. Typical examples are: too much idle chat in a meeting, sharing a video from their Facebook page, or telling lots of personal stories that don't add anything to the discussion. This person often has a favourite topic that they introduce to every situation regardless of whether it's actually relevant.

The Martyr

Mixed message: wants to communicate they are dedicated and hardworking, other people believe they are inefficient.

The positive intention of this role is the belief that if other people recognise the sacrifices they are making they will be valued and appreciated. Typical examples include working long hours as a pattern, sending emails in the dead of night, taking on other people's workload and complaining about it, bemoaning the lack of support and then refusing help.

The Mad Hatter

MAD HATTER

Mixed message: wants to be involved in many things but their contribution is undervalued by others because of their behaviour.

This is somebody who believes they can do more than they actually can and says yes to too many things. The problem results from issues with their prioritisation and time sort. Behaviours include always being late, leaving one meeting early to go to another, constantly reorganising appointments or cancelling at the last minute.

The Headless Chicken

Mixed message: believes that by being highly active they will be productive but other people see them as disorganised and unreliable.

This role is driven by stress and overwhelm where the person believes that if they just keep going, it will be OK. Behaviours include always rushing around, being unprepared, forgetting follow-up activities and skipping training events.

The Special One

Mixed message: wants to be seen as important but other people feel devalued and lose respect for them.

This is common in people who are ambitious and want to get on. Examples of this behaviour include telling people how busy they are repeatedly, reporting all the things they've done, over-justifying their activity, ignoring communication from people they don't see as important.

Your Time Boundaries, your choice

When using your time most efficiently you should be:

- Discussing ideas or concepts you plan to do something about

- Discussing or thinking about a decision that you will actually make and commit to

- Planning, organising and prioritising your activities

- Reviewing activities with the intention of getting learning to inform your future action

- Undertaking activities chosen by you for downtime like watching that TV programme you love, reading a good book, meditating, exercise etc.

You can now decide what you want to change.

This could include:

- Giving important things or people your undivided attention

- Reducing time with people you value less, drain your energy or don't value you

- Stop complaining about things you secretly like doing

- Start being enthusiastic about things you enjoy

- Answering your phone when certain people call

- Not answering your phone when some other people call

- Deciding on a 'please come and talk to me' and a 'leave me alone' signal for work. You can do this using your posture and body language. It's the smart equivalent of putting your headphones on. People soon learn when you are available and when you are not.

If you aren't sure what signals you are giving off and how your signals are received by others, ask some trusted colleagues or friends. If they know you genuinely want the feedback they will usually be very open. People are often amazed at the signals their faces and body language give off that they weren't intending. You can then practise doing something that gives off the message you want others to receive.

Beware the Boundary Violators

Riya was a popular member of staff but found that her time was being hijacked by people who kept distracting her with their personal stories, complaints or gossip. She hated being rude so just let them talk and showed some sympathy for their situation. She found she was working late too often and her family were paying the price of her being too nice.

To behave her Time Boundaries better, she decided to be proactive in saying *hello* and asking people how they were when it suited her, at lunch time, so that she could still maintain good relationships. She developed a more purposeful walk around the office when she didn't want to be caught, avoiding eye contact and started answering her phone if someone was at her desk talking, or pulling her things together as if off for a meeting. She also deferred people who popped over for idle chat, suggesting they catch up later or after work, knowing they would come back if it was important.

With these small changes she found she was able to finish work on time a few nights a week and keep her relationships with her colleagues.

Summary

What have you learned in this chapter?

- You communicate your boundaries in your behaviour.

- Others respond to this behaviour.

- You need to become aware of behaviour and which of the roles you are likely to adopt.

- With this awareness you can then decide what to change.

Action: Here are the first steps we suggest you take towards clearly behaving your Time Boundaries and taking control of your time.

- Become aware of what Time Boundaries you are communicating.

- Which one of the roles do you most relate to?

- What is there to learn from what you have identified?

- Is there an unhelpful pattern that you can work on?

For the next 7 days, in meetings, when talking to others or at home think about your Time Boundaries and identify:

- The situations where you feel your behaviour is giving the message you're intending and the results you get as a consequence.

- The situations where you feel you are not giving the message you are intending and the results you get as a consequence.

At the end of the 7 days, from what you have identified, what one step can you take to help you create clarity with others on your Time Boundaries?

You may decide that you will be on time for every meeting and event for the next week.

You may want to do more of the activities that you have identified as improving the utilisation of your time resource.

One way to help bring Time Boundaries to your awareness is to notice it in others. The next time you are in a meeting or out for dinner with friends pay attention to what people are saying about their time and how they are behaving it. Notice who is always late for the meeting, or dinner. Who is always telling anyone who will listen that they are busy and who is always rearranging meetings?

CHAPTER 9

Communicate Your Time Boundaries (Part II): Language

"Language is the means by which we negotiate our relationship with time."

Romesh Gunesekera

The words you use are as important as your behaviour in setting appropriate Time Boundaries. They tell other people what and who you value and if they can control you and your time.

There are key instances in our day-to-day communication where simple changes in language can make a big difference.

The four simple things to focus on are:

1. How to respond to other people's requests for your time.

2. How to ask others for their time.

3. The watch outs when responding to requests for your time or asking people for their time.

4. The language of your time.

1. How to respond to other people's requests for your time

People often have a standard response to these requests.

- You might be someone who agrees to everything and then worries about how you will do it all.

- You might respond with something vague so that the other person can't pin you down by saying something like, 'I'll try to…' or 'I'll do my best to…'

- You may be someone whose initial response to everything is, "Give me a minute" or "I can't just now because…" or "I'm busy".

It's not that any of these responses are wrong in themselves. They don't work for every request. The best approach, and the one that will help you master time, is to have choice in your response to requests for your time.

There are three standard responses:

Saying *Yes*

This response tells others that you are always available and they will expect you to be so.

Your intention may be to be helpful, accommodating and friendly.

If this is your pattern you may find that other people don't respect your time or take up too much of it. If you say *yes* they will keep on asking and expect you to say *yes*. It can lead to you feeling you are only there for others and afraid to change your response for fear of offending.

Saying *No* or *I'm too busy*

This response pushes other people away. They will eventually stop asking you, even for things you might want to do.

Your intention may be to be clear, avoid being dumped on and to be in control of your own time.

If this is your pattern, over time you may stop being invited to things you would have liked to go to. People you care about may drop out of your life because you've unintentionally told them they are not important enough for you. In your career you may be seen as unapproachable, inflexible or even inefficient and too busy to be given more responsibility. If that is your intention then great, if not it could have an unintended impact on your relationships and your career.

Saying nothing

Being vague in your responses to people's requests for your time, you are telling them not to rely on you.

Your intention may be to be flexible, be available to help without being tied down and you may even be unsure yourself.

If this is your pattern, it may lead to mistrust in important relationships as people do not know where they stand with you. In a work situation the good roles will go elsewhere because your boss may not feel that you can be relied upon or are pro-active enough for the role.

To have Time Mastery you require choice in the way in which you respond to these requests

Saying it clearly

When someone makes a request for your time it is just that. You can consider each request on its own merit each time it is made. That way you can say *yes* to something one day and *no* to it the next as it fits for you in your life.

Push the pause button on your normal response and be clear on whether you actually want to do the thing that has been requested of you. The way you do this is:

STEP 1

Identify your own signals

Think back over work or personal situations when you've been asked to do things or when you've been invited to things.

- Are you aware of your internal signal, a feeling or thought that indicates to you the things you would say *yes* straight away to, the 'no-brainers' of the time world? These could be things you love doing or things you consider to be important.

- Are you aware of your internal signal for 'no way', a feeling or thought which signals to you that you would rather cut your right arm off than do this thing? These could be things you dislike doing or requests from people you don't like or overburden you.

- Are you aware of your internal signal for 'need to think about that'? A feeling or a thought that this might be a big ask, or something involving more than is immediately obvious? These might be situations where buying yourself some time to think it through is useful.

Everyone has these signals. Get in touch with yours and identify which activities, requests and people hit which responses.

STEP 2

Consider the consequences

Consider these two questions:

1. What are the consequences of doing or not doing the thing requested?

2. Am I OK with those consequences?

It is important to accurately consider the consequences of saying *yes* or *no* or nothing.

Saying *no* could ultimately lead to a great opportunity or saying *no* might have an impact on your career.

Saying *yes* might have complications you haven't anticipated, or you might be training people inadvertently to take advantage of you.

You can only do one thing at a time so by saying *yes* to something you are saying *no* to something else you could be doing. What else could you be doing and is it OK to do this instead? Saying *yes* often needs a little bit more thought than people want to give it or believe they have the right to do.

STEP 3

Decide your response

Think about how you will communicate a clear, assertive, respectful response.

Responding appropriately involves:

1. Acknowledging and respecting the person's request

2. Giving them a clear answer

3. Giving a clear next step.

Examples of good ways to say *Yes*

'That's sounds brilliant/ interesting/ important. I'd be delighted/ happy to. What specifically do you need from me?'

'Thanks for asking me. I'd love to be involved. Give me some more detail so that I can get a sense of the part I'll play.'

'Thanks for inviting me. It sounds great. I'm in. Where is it? What time?'

Examples of good ways to say *No*

'I understand that's an important piece of work. I've got other things of similar priority that need doing at the moment that means I won't be able to start it for a few weeks. I'm sorry.'

'Thanks for thinking of me. I'm at capacity at the moment so will have to say *no* on this occasion. I wish you all the best with the project.'

'Thanks for inviting me, it's not really my thing so best to count me out on this occasion. I hope you have a great time.'

Examples of good ways to buy yourself time

'That sounds fascinating. Part of me just wants to jump in and say *yes* but with my sensible head on I'll need a few days to think it through. I don't want to start something I can't fully engage in. I'll get back to you by Friday.'

'I understand that's a really important piece of work. I want to think it through before committing either way. When's the latest I can get back to you?'

'I love the sound of that. Let me check it out this end and I'll let you know in the next few days. Can you send me through the details?'

2. How to ask others for their time

In any request for someone else's time, you need to understand that they have the right to say *no*. Fear of rejection prevents so many people from asking for what they want, when all they are really fearing is the word *no*. In a healthy relationship people have the freedom to say *no*. When someone says *no* it doesn't mean they don't like you or don't value you, they have simply decided *no* to this thing on this occasion.

You can reduce the chances of someone saying *no* or saying *yes* and then not doing it by asking them appropriately.

You ask someone for their time appropriately when you:

1. Demonstrate respect for them in your request.

2. Present the request in a way that connects for them.

3. Ask specifically for what you want.

Examples of good ways to ask people for their time

- 'When I saw this project I thought of you, I know how great you are at working through the details. Would you like to support me on this one?'

- 'I've been asked to go to a late meeting next week which is important for me. Would you look after the children until 9pm? It's a school night and they really need a calm influence and routine which you always give them.'

- 'Help I'm getting lost on the detail with this piece of work! You are great at the bigger picture. Can I buy you a coffee and you help me sort out my thoughts?'

When asking for help people often spend too much time over-explaining why they need help rather than connecting it to the person they are asking. The other person is rarely that interested in your mountain of paperwork so instead respect them and think about what they will get out of it.

This could be a chance to:

- Use a particular skill they have

- Get extra recognition or reward

- Make a contribution to the family

- Improve themselves or build on their skills

- Influence something they might not otherwise be able to

- Make an impact

- Make new friends or connections

- Help out a dear friend

- Get their teeth into something complex

Not everyone will get excited by all of these things, so when asking for other people's time, think about what floats their boat, rather than asking in terms of what would motivate you.

Showing respect for the person is not the same as grovelling. Notice in all the examples there's no apology for asking. If you begin with an apology you are basically putting the task, yourself and the other person down before you ask. Show respect by appreciating them and their skills rather than apologising for asking for their time.

3. Watch outs when responding to requests for your time or asking people for their time

- Be clear and to the point in your request or your response. Avoid waffle and words that indicate woolliness like perhaps, kind of, maybe, probably.

- Be real. Don't say, 'I'd love to' if you don't mean it. People pick up on incongruous communication even if you think you've got away with it.

- Don't put the blame elsewhere; like blaming your partner, boss or children's needs as the reason you cannot do what they are asking. If it is not clear and assertive the other person may think there is room to argue or negotiate and you end up in an argument or over-justifying yourself. It can also come across as weak.

- Don't be tempted to over-explain yourself. They don't need it and you don't need to justify your decision to someone else. If the other person wants more information they can ask you a question.

- Be careful with using the word 'but' when asking for and dealing with requests for time. The word 'but' linguistically deletes the first part of the sentence so if you say, 'That sounds great but…' you are basically saying that doesn't sound great at all. The other person will pick this up unconsciously. Instead of 'but' use 'and' or put in a full stop at the end of "That sounds great." and then go on to explain why you can't or won't do it.

- Be careful of using the word 'try' when asking for or dealing with requests for time. Try doesn't really mean anything. If you use it you are in danger of giving a message you had not intended. Try is a cop-out word and one very common in most people's language so be careful about using it. If you ask someone for their time and they say they will 'try', ask them what would stop them or what they would need to be able to do it. This will give you a clearer idea of whether they are really saying *yes* or *no*.

4. The language of your time

If you were to record your daily dialogue you would be amazed at how much time-related language you use. Even using words like 'first', 'next' and 'now' are time related as they imply an order.

The way a person usually responds to the question, 'How was your day?' gives a clear indication of how well they communicate their Time Boundaries.

- If someone's answer to the question is something like 'chaos' or 'hectic', what image, thought or feeling springs to your mind? What does it make you think about how well this person communicates their Time Boundaries and uses their time resource?

- If instead they said, 'There was a lot going on and I achieved what I wanted to achieve' what image, thought or feeling springs to your mind? What does it make you think about how well this person communicates their Time Boundary and uses their time resource?

How do you usually respond to the question, 'How was your day?'

The language of your time has two important functions:

1. It sets clear Time Boundaries with other people and helps train them how to treat you.

2. It impacts how you think and feel about your time. The words you use will create pictures in your head, sounds in your mind and feelings. The question is, are they helpful to you or not?

Think about the words you commonly use to describe your day and how you are spending your time.

Ask yourself is this how you want people to see you?

Teaching Team Time Boundaries

Matt leads a large team of architects. Their main time-wasting problems were in how they communicated. He discovered that they almost always said *yes* to clients, were vague with developers and said *no* frequently to their colleagues.

This was causing a lot of rework and strained relations within the practice. At an away day, Matt worked with them to set up some general boundaries for clients, developers and colleagues, the general rules of the road, what's the agreed line so that everyone could be clear about what they could say and be backed up on and be able to follow through on. They were clear rules but general ones; exceptions could be made but before being made they would need further discussion within the team before being agreed.

They practised for a month and then reconvened to work through any problems or anomalies. The practice is now much more efficient, productive and profitable.

Summary

What have you learned in this chapter?

- You communicate your boundaries in your language.

- Others respond to this language.

- Overly fixed or overly flexible boundaries can create unintended issues.

- When someone asks you for your time, it is a request.

- You can say *yes*, *no* or *maybe*.

- When you ask someone for their time, be clear what you want from them.

Action: Become aware of your language. What is your normal language around time? Do you always say *yes* or *no* or *maybe* when asked for your time.

For the next 7 days identify:

- People who do not respect your Time Boundaries or ask for more than you are willing to give.

- The situations where you feel you are being clear and the results you get as a consequence.

- The situations where you feel you are not being clear and the results you get as a consequence.

What simple change to your language will help you create clarity with others?

You may want to stop doing things that waste your time and do not add value to what you want to achieve. That may involve practising saying *no* more than you currently do.

You may want to do more of the activities that you have identified as improving the utilisation of your time resource. That may involve clearly asking someone else to help you with something or perhaps saying *yes* to more things than you currently do.

Your time is exactly that, yours. It's up to you to make that clear to everyone

PART C

A New Relationship with Time

CHAPTER 10

Your Steps to Time Mastery

"Have a bias toward action – let's see something happen now. You can break that big plan into small steps and take the first step right away."

Indira Gandhi

Successful people in any walk of life whether it be business, sport or life in general differ from others in one key respect. They not only know something, they do something with that knowledge to help them succeed.

Applying the tools and techniques you have learned in this book will allow you to do the best you can in all the important areas of your life, not rush a job just to get it done or waste time on things that do not improve the output.

Think small steps

Start somewhere and start small. One of the reasons change is difficult is that you look to change too much too quickly.

Long-lasting sustainable change doesn't happen overnight. If you've ever tried the latest fad diet you'll know that. You might lose some weight fast but unless you design healthy habits for yourself, you will soon return to your former self. You might go on a meditation retreat, come back feeling all balanced and relaxed and then two days later you are back shouting at the kids and running around late for your next meeting.

Successful and happy people develop healthy life habits by making small incremental changes towards what they want.

Time Mastery is no different; it's a healthy life habit.

Combined with small steps, a disciplined process gives you and those around you time to become familiar and comfortable with the changes you are making. It will provide evidence of progress and will give you the enthusiasm to continue.

It is not only possible to do this, it is easier to achieve than you think.

Pathway to Time Mastery

The key is to get started. There are two pathways you can choose. Which one you take depends on where you are starting from and what your most pressing time issues or your key goals are.

Pathway One: The Integration Method

This approach is good for you if you prefer to take action and then assimilate it before doing more. It's a way of making progress quickly, by picking and choosing your priorities as they come up or suit you. It's also a great one if you get bored easily or are very busy juggling many things. You can break it down into small tasks and goals so you don't get overwhelmed.

STEP 1

Start with an easy win

The best way to convince your brain that you are making progress is to find some quick wins that you can implement easily and that will have a positive impact. Pick one or two of the Time Wasters from Chapter 4 and begin working on those. You could:

- Work on closing those open loops

- Develop clear outcomes for what you are doing

- Challenge some of your unhelpful beliefs around time

Developing useful habits is an important part of taking this pathway. Only work on one or two at a time and master those before moving on.

STEP 2

Take one of the Four Keys to Time Mastery and master it

Pick the one you feel you can most easily tackle in the first round and in the next round you can pick the one that seems most difficult next. This order is important.

To train your brain for success you first need to know what success looks, feels and sounds like, hence picking the one you feel most confident about first.

STEP 3

Integrate with Life Resources

- How have the changes you've implemented at each step positively impacted your health or your financial situation?

- Are there any unintended negative consequences impacting your health or financial situation? If so consider how to tweak the changes so that they fit better in the wider context of your life.

This is a less active stage of the pathway and essential. Sit down once a week and think about, or jot down in your notebook the progress you have made. If you are working through this book with a buddy, get together for a coffee once a month to talk it through and keep each other on track.

STEP 4

Review feedback and select the next easy win

Review the output of Steps 1 to 3.

- What have you learned about your own style and attitude to time?

- What changes will you make to your process?

- Based on the output, what next easy win will you choose?

Once you have taken the learning from the feedback, go back to Step 1.

Pathway Two: The Stairway Method

This pathway is good for you if you like to work in a systematic way as you'll be taking a step-by-step approach to all the elements in turn. If you are integrating it into a corporate training programme this is probably the best way to apply it as most people are successful with this approach when they have guidance and someone to keep them on track.

STEP 1

Identify the issues to work on

Work through Part A of the book and note your thoughts and learnings at each stage. Part A is all about getting your head around the concepts, so don't commit to any action at this stage. Make notes which might include:

- Which of the Life Resources you are too focussed on (Chapter 2)

- Which of the Life Resources you are neglecting (Chapter 2)

- Time Myths you live your life by, either all of the time or in certain contexts like work or with family (Chapter 3)

- Time Wasters you engage in (Chapter 4)

Look at the common themes in your notes. Ideally discuss them with someone you trust and get their perspective on it. Identify two or three themes you want to focus on as you work through the Four Keys to Time Mastery.

STEP 2

Master the Four Keys of Time Mastery

Work through each of the Four Keys in turn. They are ordered this way in the book not by importance but because the order suits most learning styles. As you work through each chapter, bring in your themes from Part A and use them to decide what to work through. Leave each chapter with three or four actions and go and practise them. When you have achieved your actions for each chapter then move onto the next chapter. Some people like to take a break between each Key to allow time to integrate the actions properly and to a standard they are happy with.

STEP 3

Build for the future

Review your learnings and successes and create a plan for the next six months for continuous improvement.

It's better with friends

Whatever pathway you choose, it really helps, particularly if you are not doing a programme or being coached, if you buddy up with someone. This could be a friend or a group of friends, your book club or even a group of colleagues at work.

It's easy to go off track or lose your way when you do anything alone. It's like training for a marathon or preparing for a big exam; it's easier, more successful and more fun if you work with someone else. Arrange to meet up regularly and check on each other's progress, set goals and actions and offer suggestions of support.

Choose your path and start walking

Success requires you to take yourself a little out of your comfort zone (otherwise you'll only be doing what you already do) but not so much that you feel overwhelmed or out of your depth.

Whatever route you choose, a programme, one-to-one coaching or the pathways we've outlined above, the important thing is to begin. Success breeds success and confidence grows as you see the positive impact of the action you are taking.

CHAPTER 11

A New Relationship with Life

*"In the end, it's not the years in your life that count.
It's the life in your years."*

Abraham Lincoln

What does a satisfying and fulfilling life actually look like to you?

You can't even think about this question until some of the most pressing problems in your life have been resolved. If it's a mystery to you at the moment don't worry; once you have resolved the immediate problems be they Time, Money, Health or relationship related, your mind will have space to explore this.

- You will reach a point when your pressing time-related problems are resolved or put into context.

- You will feel less conflicted and pulled in different directions.

- You will feel more in control of your day-to-day activities.

- You will have more choice of how to spend your time.

- There will be space in your mind for thinking, 'What do I want to do with my life now?' and a belief that you have the time to do it.

Creating a satisfying and fulfilling life

There are six essential steps to this:

1. Don't get too specific

2. Don't look for Utopia

3. Try things out

4. Create a vision board

5. Think and plan long term; act now

6. Decide what you need to succeed

STEP 1

Don't get too specific

People often think they are looking for the 'one thing' they have to be or do to fulfil their purpose in life. This is too specific and can either make you feel despondent that you've missed your opportunity or that you're too late to start now. This is because you are trying to hone in on one thing rather than thinking about your general direction.

If you know what you want in general terms, you will find there are many ways to achieve that.

The key is to begin. Movement creates energy and energy can help you to feel that you are moving forward. It is easier to make small adjustments to the direction of travel when you are moving than when you are still.

STEP 2

Don't look for Utopia

People often discard their hopes and dreams because they can't have perfection.

You might feel that your calling is to go and teach children in Africa but in reality that might not be possible because of family commitments at home or a clash with other priorities.

That doesn't mean you can't contribute or fulfil part of that wish.

Embrace compromise and as a result you will have much of the life you want and be living your life with purpose.

Find someone with whom you can discuss your dreams, however out there and whacky the dream may be. When people keep their hopes and dreams all locked up inside they become sad and resentful.

If you can air them and discuss them, the ideas and collective creativity that comes might surprise you.

A Fulfilled Life

Sarah is a talented sports person and photographer and she could probably just about make a living doing these things. Rather than quitting her job she compromised, contracting for 6 months of the year and spending the other 6 months doing the stuff she loves. She can enjoy and put all her energy into her sport and photography knowing that financially things are taken care of.

STEP 3

Try things out

You can't create a good life by just thinking about it; you have to actually do something. Some people end up in a dream world because they just think and dream and think and dream but don't take any steps or try anything out.

That's a bit like watching the football on the TV and imagining you are a world class striker; unless you get off the sofa you won't stand a chance!

Our bodies are designed to 'experience' things. Only by giving something a go can you get a sense of what you love and what's not right for you. As they say in the army 'Time spent on a rekkie is never wasted', so shadowing someone, doing a short internship, taking a sabbatical (whilst you still have a job you can go back to) or investing time developing a skill is all part of this.

STEP 4

Create a vision board

Creating a vision board of all the things that you love, could love and think you might love is a great way to get a clearer sense of your new relationship with life. It will help programme your mind to look for opportunities at the same time. Here's how you do it:

- Collect up a load of magazines

- Look through them for interesting pictures or words that speak to you

- Cut them out and arrange and glue them on a piece of paper or card.

- Step back and review your vision. What does it tell you?

If you are very artistic you could draw or create a 3D model, for most of the human race though, paper and glue is more than adequate.

STEP 5

Think and plan long term; act now

You know the story, the hare was faster and ran about here and there in a mad fashion, whereas the tortoise moved slowly and deliberately and eventually won the race.

When it comes to time be a tortoise; keep moving, slowly and deliberately in the direction you want to go to. Sometimes short cuts will appear, but think very carefully before taking one, as there may be consequences.

Once you know the general direction of your life, even if the idea is quite vague at first, you need to start taking steps towards it.

You don't need to have it all mapped out. It's important to be thinking a couple of steps ahead of where you are, but not every step. There are a few reasons for this:

- If you're clear on your general direction, you won't be blown off course by irrelevancies and distractions.

- By thinking two or three steps ahead, you always have a plan, but you are open to be flexible if you want or need to. For example a man might have a plan to go and live abroad, and then his wife gets pregnant. This is something that will make them stop, consider and discuss as a couple whether now is the right time to do this. It might still be or they might need to adjust their timings in light of the new information.

- People who stick narrowly to their well-defined path to their goal tend to miss opportunities to enrich it and make it better.

STEP 6

Decide what you need to succeed

Whatever it is that will make a satisfying and fulfilling life for you, think about what you need that will set you up for success in the future. Do you need to:

- Save money to give you some cash reserves for your future business venture?

- Learn some new skills or get a qualification?

- Get into some new circles and meet some like-minded people?

- Begin to get acquainted with a place or certain part of the world?

- Try out your bucket list of 'maybes'?

- Begin to build your profile as an expert in a certain profession?

Whatever you want to do, begin now.

CHAPTER 12

Over to You

"You must take personal responsibility. You cannot change the circumstances, the seasons, or the wind, but you can change yourself. That is something you have charge of."

Jim Rohn

What are you going to do now? What have you learned in the book that is going to be your starting point?

We want you to live your own satisfying and fulfilling life and we are happy to help you where we can. The book is the start, and you can choose where you want to go next.

Each chapter is full of information, ideas and suggested actions that you can take. Not all of it will be relevant to you at this stage of your life, but some of it will be more important and relevant right now. Reflect now on what resonated for you in what we have said. Where did you say to yourself, 'That's me', 'I need to do that more' or even

'Why on earth would you do that?' Whatever it was that stood out for you is probably a good place to start.

Stand out from the crowd, be different and take control of how you spend your time. Decide that you want more from your time and your life and commit to making a plan, investing the time and putting in the effort, to use your Time resource to deliver the success and joy in life that you talk about.

Review the Table of Contents for the book and answer the following questions:

- What are the main ideas and concepts that connected and stood out for you as you read each chapter?

- Can you now think of Time as a resource that is yours to control?

- Which Time Wasters can you begin to eliminate from your life right now?

- Which of the Four Keys to Time Mastery will have the biggest positive impact on your time and your life now?

- As you read this, are you saying, 'Yes, but...' If so, what is getting in your way?

- Do you know anyone that you could buddy up with to implement the ideas and actions in the book?

Thank you for using your time resource to read this book. We wish you well in taking back control of your time. We would love to hear how you get on and we would really appreciate your feedback and comments on the book. We are also real people behind this book so please get in touch via any of the contact routes at the end of the book to ask questions or for more support and information.

"We must use time wisely and forever realise that the time is always ripe to do right."

Nelson Mandela

About the Authors

John McLachlan & Karen Meager

Before they set up Monkey Puzzle Training & Consultancy in 2007, Karen and John both had successful careers in business. Karen worked in the fund management industry in London and John was a chartered accountant in practice and financial director on the board of a number of companies.

Whilst studying for her MBA Karen became fascinated by the psychological make up of people who are great at what they do and used her knowledge to recruit and train for all types of roles in her organisation, from call centres and sales, to leaders. John had always been more interested in the people behind the numbers than accountancy itself. He used this knowledge blended with his strategic expertise to help businesses and business owners be successful and live more fulfilling lives.

Karen and John take the latest scientific and academic thinking and make it accessible and usable in everyday life and work. Clinically qualified in psychotherapy and hypnotherapy, they are also two of only a handful of NLP Master Trainers in the UK.

At Monkey Puzzle Karen, John and their team specialise in leadership development and supporting people in their personal and professional growth. Their first book *Real Leaders for the Real World* received five star reviews and was awarded finalist in the International Book Awards.

Contact Details

Karen Meager

karen@monkeypuzzletraining.co.uk

John McLachlan

john@monkeypuzzletraining.co.uk

Monkey Puzzle Training & Consultancy Limited

www.monkeypuzzletraining.co.uk

f @monkeypuzzletraining

𝕏 @monkeypuzzle_